American Photographers of the Depression

Sam Garrett

American Photographers of the Depression

Farm Security Administration Photographs 1935-1942

Introduction by Charles Hagen

Thames and Hudson

First published in Great Britain in 1991 by
Thames and Hudson Ltd, London
Originally published in France by Centre National de la Photographie
Copyright © 1982 by Centre National de la Photographie, Paris
Text copyright © 1983 by Charles Hagen
Text by James Agee from 'Let Us Now Praise Famous Men'
Copyright 1939 and 1940 by James Agee
Copyright renewed 1969 by Mia Fritsch Agee
Reprinted by permission of Houghton Mifflin Company

Printed and bound in Italy

FSA : at first this breezy acronym referred simply to the Farm Security Administration, one of the many programs propounded in the 1930s by President Franklin D. Roosevelt and his advisors to combat the Great Depression. But today, through the work of a handful of photographers employed by a minor subdivision within the agency, the name FSA has come not only to evoke the full ravages of the Depression and the optimism of the New Deal, but also to represent one of the most ambitious attempts ever made to depict a society in photographs. For many of us the image we have of America in the '30s is based on the photographs of such FSA photographers as Walker Evans, Dorothea Lange and Russell Lee, who, under the often imperious direction of Roy Stryker, worked with one eye on the ferment of the day and the other on the broader patterns of history.

The Historical Unit—as this photographic section was officially named—was formed in 1935 as part of the newly-established Resettlement Administration. (Two years later the name of the agency was changed into Farm Security Administration.) In the summer of that year Stryker, an instructor in the economics department at Columbia University, in New York, was asked to join the RA by Rexford Tugwell, his mentor at Columbia and the head of the new agency.

The Resettlement Administration was a centerpiece of the New Deal's agricultural policies.[1] The Depression had blighted nearly every sector of the American economy, but none so severely as the nation's farms. Throughout the 1920s a variety of factors had driven farm prices down and forced many farmers—especially those working small holdings—into desperate poverty. By 1929 nearly eight million people in farm areas lived on the edge of subsistence. Among the hardest hit were tenant farmers and sharecroppers, who worked land they did not own and were therefore more apt to ignore soil-conservation precautions–thus quickly exhausting the land. (Sharecroppers, as the name suggests, divided their harvests with the owner of the property they farmed, while tenant farmers included those who paid their rent in cash.) Up to 75 percent of all farms in the South and Southwest were operated by tenant farmers in this period. As the Depression wore on many were forced to leave their holdings and to move around the country looking for migrant work of any sort. The existence of this army of Okies (short for Oklahoma, though they came from many other states as well) strongly dramatized the plight of the small farmer to urban Americans.

This was the situation the Resettlement Administration was formed to combat. Its hodgepodge of programs included offering low-interest loans to farmers to allow them to buy better land; sponsoring soil conservation programs; and undertaking such "resettlement" projects as experimental communal farms and camps for migrant farm workers. Like many other New Deal programs, the RA's ambitious projects were both controversial and untested, and so it was no surprise that Tugwell, one of Roosevelt's closest advisors and an expert in agricultural economics, should be named to head it. At Columbia, Tugwell had come to understand the value of photographs in dramatizing economic arguments and analyses, and his book *American Economic Life and the Means of its Improvement* (1925), written with Thomas Munro, included photographs on nearly every page. It was thus logical that when Tugwell took over the Resettlement Administration he should call on Stryker–who as a graduate student had gathered the illustrations for that pioneering volume–to come to Washington to record and publicize the activities of the new agency.

Stryker brought a familiarity with both rural life and photography to his new position. Born in 1893, he had been raised in Colorado, where he had briefly tried his hand at cattle ranching before heading to New York in 1921. There he enrolled at Columbia, where he remained–first as a student and later as an instructor–until he went to Washington. Through his picture research on *American Economic Life* and other projects, Stryker had become familiar with the work of Jacob Riis, Lewis Hine, and other earlier photographers who had used the medium both to record aspects of their society and to champion specific social reforms. (In fact, Hine–then an old man–had provided over a third of the pictures used in *American Economic Life.*)

And so Stryker went to Washington. His first months at the Resettlement Administration were spent assembling a staff of photographers. Arthur Rothstein, a former student of Stryker's who had printed work on various projects for him, came down from Columbia to take charge of setting up a darkroom and handling the technical end of the new section's work. Carl Mydans, a former journalist who had been working in another New Deal agency as a photographer, transferred into Stryker's unit. Walker Evans, a young New York photographer whose stately, transparently metaphoric large-format photographs of architecture and urban scenes had begun to attract the attention of the art world, was hired by Stryker in October. Ben Shahn, a painter who had shared a house with Evans in New York, was employed by a different division of the FSA, but Stryker obtained copies of a remarkable series of photographs Shahn had made on a three-month trip through the South in the fall of 1935, and those images formed an important part of the Historical Unit's nascent files. In the 1920s Dorothea Lange had been a successful San Francisco portrait photographer, but faced with the disruption of the Depression she had begun to record the unemployed and migrant workers drawn to the West by the illusory promise of work. The photographs Lange made to accompany a 1935 report on relief efforts in California came to Stryker's attention, and he promptly hired her as the unit's West Coast representative. It was to be the following spring, though, before Lange would have the chance to travel to Washington and meet Stryker.

This remarkable group of photographers–along with Russell Lee, trained as a painter, who was hired when Mydans left in 1936 to join the staff of the new *Life* magazine–formed the core of the RA–and later of the FSA–photography unit. During the seven years of the project all but Lee would leave the group–Evans in 1937, Lange at the end of 1939, Rothstein in 1940. Other photographers were hired: Marion Post Wolcott, who joined the unit late in 1938; Jack Delano and John Vachon (who had worked as a clerk in the group's Washington offices), both hired in 1940; and John Collier Jr., taken on in 1941. The young Gordon Parks, later a well-known *Life* photographer, served an internship with the group in 1941. (Two other photographers hired as part of the initial staff, Theo Jung and Paul Carter, served only a very short time with the unit.) All told, barely more than a dozen photographers ever worked for the division; at times the tiny staff numbered only two or three photographers. But it is primarily on the work of that first astonishing collection of talents–Evans, Lange, Shahn, Lee, Rothstein, Mydans–that the reputation of FSA rests.

The working procedure developed by Stryker and his team was a simple but effective one. Photographers would be sent out from Washington on shooting trips, lasting sometimes for months at a time. They would be given lists of specific subjects throughout the region they would be visiting; these would commonly include various examples of RA- (or FSA-) sponsored projects, to be photographed for straightforward publicity purposes. Or photographers might be sent to cover a natural disaster, especially if it affected agency projects and was deemed newsworthy by Stryker and the staff in Washington. For example, when the Ohio and Mississippi Rivers flooded in early 1937, Evans was sent to the Lower Mississippi to photograph the resulting devastation, while Lee covered the effects of the flooding in the Ohio River Valley. In addition to these specific assignments, photographers would be asked to cover general situations as well–drought conditions in a certain region, say. Before photographers would go out on these assignments, Stryker would provide them with a broad range of background material–economic, historical, sociological–about the region they were to visit. Each photographer was asked to buy a copy of J. Russell Smith's *North America,* a detailed, section-by-section study of the social and economic characteristics of the continent, and they would be given maps, pamphlets, and other books to read as well. These published references would be supplemented by detailed conversations with Stryker and others about the situations to be photographed. When the photographers were in the field Stryker would write them long letters telling them of additional picture needs and assessing the photographs they were sending back to Washington. (Such letters were of particular importance in Lange's case, since she was based on the West Coast and seldom visited Washington.).

Sometimes the lists of shots given to the photographers would take the form of elaborate "shooting scripts."The most famous of these grew out of a luncheon Stryker had in New

York in the spring of 1936 with Robert Lynd, author of *Middletown*, the landmark sociological study of small-town America. Stryker showed Lynd some of the photographs made by the unit, and the two men discussed ways in which the project could be used to portray not only agricultural problems, but rural and small-town life in general. On the train back to Washington after their long meeting, Stryker drew up a detailed outline of the topics they had discussed, which was later elaborated into a shooting script listing "things which should be photographed as an American background." The script suggested typical activities of people in various economic classes that might be examined, from listening to the radio and playing bridge at home in the evening to attending church and gathering with other people—in country clubs and lodges, for the well-to-do, and in beer halls, pool halls, saloons, and on street corners, for the poor. Only one item referred specifically to events of the day: "The effect of the Depression in the smaller towns in the United States."[2]

Shooting scripts such as this demonstrate the dual focus the photography of the Resettlement Administration quickly acquired. In the first months of the Historical Unit's existence, it had concentrated on recording specific problems, as well as providing publicity photographs of agency projects. But in the field the photographers had a great deal of freedom to cover whatever they considered noteworthy. Evans, Lange, and Lee, among others, had all been concerned with depicting aspects of American vernacular culture before they joined the Historical Unit; Stryker's sociological bent helped to shape and direct an interest each had been pursuing anyway. And it is primarily for this sociological dimension, expressed through the skilled perception of an unparalleled group of photographers, that we remember FSA today.

The work of the photographic section was carried out against a background of bureaucratic maneuvering and political pressure, with the project's budget in constant jeopardy and its existence repeatedly threatened by forces both inside and outside the government. In August, 1936, the group was embroiled in a partisan controversy over the truthfulness of its photographs. That spring Arthur Rothstein had discovered the sun-bleached skull of a steer lying on a parched patch of barren soil beside a road in North Dakota; he'd photographed it, then moved it a few feet away, to the edge of a grassy knoll, where he'd photographed it again. That fall a local newspaper published examples of both versions of the image under the headline: "It's a Fake." The story, with its tantalizing whiff of scandal, was reprinted by newspapers throughout the country. Although Stryker's staff quickly denied the charges of fakery, the controversy only gradually died down.

Soon thereafter Stryker and the Historical Unit suffered a series of bureaucratic shocks. At the end of 1936, Tugwell announced he was leaving government service, and Stryker lost a powerful ally within the agency. The following year brought a major reshuffling of the agency, as the Resettlement Administration–which until then had been an independent agency within the government–was incorporated into the Department of Agriculture, and its name changed to the one it is remembered by: the Farm Security Administration.

The conflicts with forces outside the photographic section paralleled disputes within the group itself, especially those between Stryker and Evans. Evans, designated the unit's senior photographer, preferred to work at his own pace and according to his own methods, rather than follow the explicit directives Stryker would sometimes give other members of the staff. Stryker allowed Evans a good deal of autonomy, but he found his way of working frustrating, and nagged him to produce more pictures and to keep better records of his expenses on the road. Evans achieved a very high degree of quality in his pictures from that time: nearly half of the photographs in the monograph of his work published in 1971 by the Museum of Modern Art in New York in 1971 were made during the eighteen months after he joined the Historical Unit late in 1935.[3] But he and Stryker did not get along, and even disagreed about which of his pictures were good and which were bad. When Evans asked for a leave of absence in July, 1936, to work with James Agee on the assignment for *Fortune* magazine that would develop into their book *Let Us Now Praise Famous Men*, it was granted. And when the photographic section's budget was cut the following summer, Stryker let Evans go. Lange, too, had disputes with Stryker about her work–she wanted to print her own negatives, while Stryker insisted she send them to Washington for processing. At the end of 1939 she was cut from the group permanently, after being laid off for long periods throughout the preceding three years because of budget cuts.[4]

Despite this hectic pattern of conflict over both politics and personalities, the photographs made by the section found a growing audience. An important part of Stryker's job was to see that the unit's photographs were distributed as widely as possible. Any magazine or other publication that wanted to use photographs made under the project could do so without charge. Social-reformist magazines like *Survey Graphic* frequently used FSA photographs, as did photography magazines and some of the newer general-audience picture magazines like *Life* and *Look*. In addition, traveling exhibitions and slide shows of the group's photographs were circulated throughout the country. Many books combining FSA photographs with texts were published during this time as well, including Archibald MacLeish's *Land of the Free* (1938) and Sherwood Anderson's *Home Town* (1941). The two unparalleled masterpieces of the genre were also produced by FSA photographers: *An American Exodus,* by Dorothea Lange and Paul Taylor, was published in 1939, and Evans' and Agee's *Let Us Now Praise Famous Men* finally appeared in 1941, five years after it was begun.

At least part of the great impact of the work of the FSA photographers can be traced to the widespread popularity at the time of the documentary form itself. In his superb study *Documentary Expression and Thirties America,* William Stott defines the documentary approach as "the presentation or representation of actual fact in a way that makes it credible and vivid[5]." Stott convincingly demonstrates that nearly every aspect of American cultural life in the '30s was influenced to a greater or lesser extent by the documentary attitude. A surprising range of work relied for its effect on the direct presentation of seemingly irrefutable facts–from the proletarian fiction of the day, in which the social and economic struggles of workers and poor people were recounted in fictionalized first-person narratives, to the "living newspapers" of the Federal Theater Project, in which economic statistics were dramatized for a general audience. These presentations were often expressed in deeply emotional terms, and argued implicitly for particular social reforms.

Documentary, as it developed in the '30s, was in many ways a dramatic form. Documentary projects like the FSA photographs often aimed at arousing fear and pity in their audiences, following Aristotle's description (in the *Poetics*) of the method of tragedy. But in these photographs the tragic flaw lies not in the character of some great hero–and not even in the noble poor whose suffering is depicted. Instead, the pictures imply that the flaw is in the society that has forced people into such a fearful and pitiable plight. The viewers of the photographs are an important element in that society, and thus bear a responsibility for the conditions the pictures show– and also have the potential to change them. This aspect of moral suasion underlies both the official purpose of the Historical Unit–to record and publicize the government's farm programs–and the sociological role Stryker and the photographers defined for it.

In the years leading up to the Second World War the direction of the Historical Unit changed significantly in a variety of ways. After 1938 Stryker grew convinced that the agency should devote more attention to positive aspects of farm life, and began to instruct his photographers accordingly. At the same time, the group began to take on photographic assignments for other government agencies to make up money lost in budget cuts. FSA photographers continued to pursue the documentary projects they were renowned for– in April, 1940, for example, Russell Lee produced an extensive study of Pie Town, New Mexico. But the changes continued. In 1940 Rothstein left to join *Look magazine*, the last member of the original staff to leave the unit. As the country began to prepare for war, the photography section's production turned to more explicitly propagandistic work, emphasizing America's strengths and virtues rather than its social problems.

After the United States entered the war in December, 1941, the FSA's budget was slashed more sharply than ever, and late in 1941 the Historical Unit was transferred to the Office of War Information. By now Stryker was left with only a skeleton staff, and when he himself resigned a year later, the unit came to an end. Before he left the government, however, Stryker arranged for the transfer of the files–about 70,000 prints and 170,000 negatives–to the Library of Congress. (Stryker had emphatically edited out another 100,000 images made in the course of the project by punching holes in the negatives.) With the coming of war many poor farmers from the South moved to the industrial cities of the North to work in defense factories– thus indirectly solving many of the problems the FSA had been formed to counter.

The brief and astonishingly productive life of the FSA photography section was marked by unending controversy and conflict. The partnership between Stryker, the social scientist and bureaucrat whom Rothstein has described as "a good manipulator[6]" and such accomplished artists as Evans and Lange proved to be extremely fruitful–but equally volatile.

In the end, though, after all the talk of intentions and methods, of personalities and politics, we come back to the photographs left by the FSA photographers. The country they depict is a remarkably consistent one: a stricken land, but one whose people retain their strength and dignity in spite of their trials. Face after face looks back at us from these pictures with an air of quiet determination. Of course, it's a fiction. Where is the anger? The despair? The America given us by the FSA is tremendously detailed and deeply evocative of the textures of a particular way of life in the United States. But the image of the people themselves is too simple, too purely noble, for our more cynical sense of truth. Whether the FSA photographic work is hailed as a farsighted examination of American society or dismissed as propaganda pretending to an impossible objectivity, though, the fact remains that for seven years the real America followed with interest the social drama presented in these pictures. That it did so suggests that its own values and ideals were well reflected in that generous mirror.

Charles Hagen.

1. In writing this brief outline of the FSA photography project's history I have relied on information from F. Jack Hurley's thorough biography of Stryker, *Portrait of a Decade: Roy Stryker and the Development of Documentary Photography in the Thirties* (Baton Rouge, Louisiana: Louisiana State University Press, 1972), as well as *In This Proud Land: America 1935-1943 As Seen in the FSA Photographs* by Stryker and Nancy Wood (New York: Galahad Books, 1973).
2. The complete shooting script is reprinted in Stryker and Wood, *In This Proud Land* p. 187.
3. John Szarkowski, introduction to *Walker Evans* (New York: The Museum of Modern Art, 1971).
4. See Robert Coles' essay in *Dorothea Lange: Photographs of a Lifetime* (Millerton, New York: Aperture, Inc., 1982).
5. William Stott, *Documentary Expression and Thirties America,*(New York: Oxford University Press, 1973), p. 14.
6. Rothstein, interviewed by Norman Schreiber, *Camera Arts*, November, 1982, vol. 2, n° 7.

'For in the immediate world, everything is to be discerned, for him who can discern it, and centrally and simply, without either dissection into science, or digestion into art, but with the whole of consciousness, seeking to perceive it as it stands: so that the aspect of a street in sunlight can roar in the heart of itself as a symphony, perhaps as no symphony can: and all of consciousness is shifted from the imagined, the revisive, to the effort to perceive simply the cruel radiance of what is.

This is why the camera seems to me, next to unassisted and weaponless consciousness, the central instrument of our time; and is why in turn I feel such rage at its misuse: which has spread so nearly universal a corruption of sight that I know of less than a dozen alive whose eyes I can trust even so much as my own.'

'If I had explained myself clearly you would realize by now that through this non-"artistic" view, this effort to suspend or destroy imagination, there opens before consciousness, and within it, a universe luminous, spacious, incalculably rich and wonderful in each detail, as relaxed and natural to the human swimmer, and as full of glory, as his breathing: and that it is possible to capture and communicate this universe not so well by any means of art as through such open terms as I am trying it under.

In a novel, a house or person has his meaning, his existence, entirely through the writer. Here, a house or a person has only the most limited of his meaning through me: his true meaning is much huger. It is that he *exists,* in actual being, as you do and as I do, and as no character of the imagination can possibly exist. His great weight, mystery, and dignity are in this fact...

James Agee

1. John Vachon. Company coal town, Kempton, West Virginia, 1939.

2. Walker Evans. Street scene, Morgantown, West Virginia, 1935.

3. Ben Shahn. Natchez, Mississippi, 1935.

4. Ben Shahn. Sunday, Scott's Run, West Virginia, 1935.

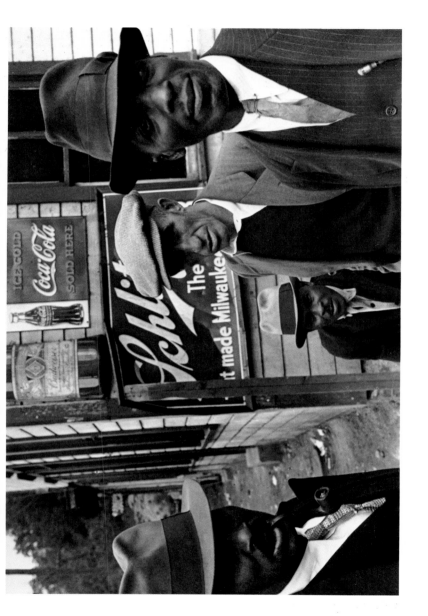

5. Ben Shahn. Main Street, Plain City, Ohio, 1938.

6. Walker Evans. Negro barbershop, Atlanta, Georgia, 1936.

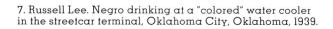
7. Russell Lee. Negro drinking at a "colored" water cooler
in the streetcar terminal, Oklahoma City, Oklahoma, 1939.

8. Russell Lee. Back of multifamily dwelling rented to negroes, Chicago, Illinois, 1941.

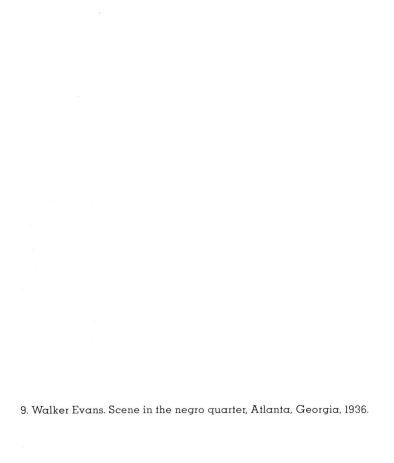

9. Walker Evans. Scene in the negro quarter, Atlanta, Georgia, 1936.

10. Walker Evans. Garage, Atlanta, Georgia, 1936.

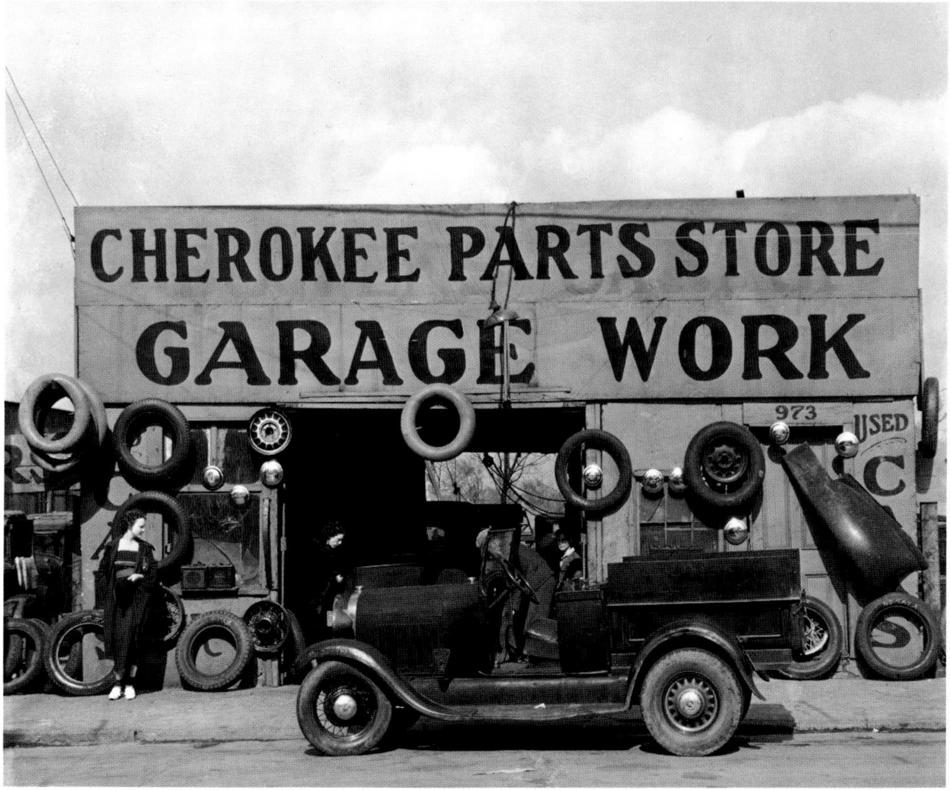
CHEROKEE PARTS STORE
GARAGE WORK
973
USED

11. Dorothea Lange. Plantation owner, Clarksdale, Mississippi, 1936.

12. Russell Lee. Second-hand tires displayed for sale,
San Marcos, Texas, 1940.

13. Walker Evans. Vicksburg, Mississippi, 1936.

14. Dorothea Lange. A mother and her two children on the road,
Tulelake, Siskiyou County, California, 1939.

15. Russell Lee. Buttermilk Junction, Martin County, Indiana, 1937.

16. Ben Shahn. Destitute Arkansas family, 1935.

17. Dorothea Lange. Sharecropper and family, 1938.

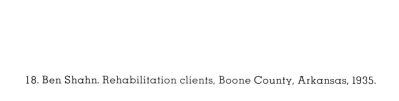
18. Ben Shahn. Rehabilitation clients, Boone County, Arkansas, 1935.

19. Dorothea Lange. Migrant mother, Nipomo, California, 1936.

20. John Vachon. Children of farmer in the Ozarks, Missouri, 1940.

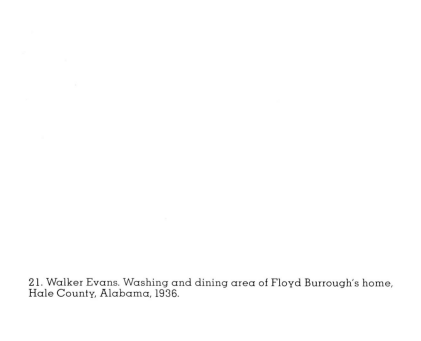

21. Walker Evans. Washing and dining area of Floyd Burrough's home, Hale County, Alabama, 1936.

22. Walker Evans. Bud Fields and his family,
Hale County, Alabama, 1936.

23. Russell Lee. Children taking a bath in their home in a community camp, Oklahoma City, Oklahoma, 1939.

24. Walker Evans. Floyd Burroughs, a cotton sharecropper,
Hale County, Alabama, 1936.

25. Jack Delano. The interior of a negro home,
Heard County, Georgia, 1941.

26. Russell Lee. Corner of a living-bedroom in cabin of negro farmer, Jefferson, Texas, 1939.

27. Russell Lee. Instruction at home, Transylvania,
Louisiana, 1939.

28. Dorothea Lange. Filipinos working in lettuce field,
Salinas, California, 1935.

29. Russell Lee. Hands of the wife of an Iowa homesteader,
Woodbury County, 1936.

30. Arthur Rothstein. Farmer and sons walking in the face
of a dust storm, Cimarron County, Oklahoma, 1936.

31. Walker Evans. Sunday singing, Frank Tengle's family,
Hale County, Alabama, 1936.

32. Walker Evans. A miner's home, vicinity Morgantown,
Scott's Run, West Virginia, 1936.

33. Russell Lee. FSA client and his sons,
Caruthersville, Missouri, 1938.

34. Russell Lee. Abandoned gold mine,
Idaho Springs, Colorado, 1941.

35. Arthur Rothstein. Building, Birmingham, Alabama, 1937.

General Outdoor Adv Co

WORLD'S HIGHEST STANDARD OF LIVING

There's no way like the American Way

36. Russell Lee. Sharecropper's son,
New Madrid County, Southeast Missouri, 1938.

37. John Vachon. Berkeley Springs, West Virginia, 1939.

38. Walker Evans. A child's grave, Hale County, Alabama, 1936.

39. Walker Evans. Roadside store, vicinity Selma, Alabama, 1935.

40. Russell Lee. Pie Town, New Mexico, 1940.

41. Russell Lee. Roadside camp of migrant workers,
Lincoln County, Oklahoma, 1939.

42. Dorothea Lange. Former Nebraska farmer, now a migrant farm worker, Klamath County, Oregon, 1939.

43. Russell Lee. Signs in front of a highway tavern,
Crystal City, Texas, 1939.

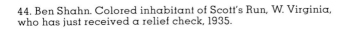

44. Ben Shahn. Colored inhabitant of Scott's Run, W. Virginia, who has just received a relief check, 1935.

45. Russell Lee. Radio with ornaments and decoration in home of FSA client, (vicinity), Caruthersville, Missouri, 1936.

46. John Vachon. Country doctor examining child in farm house,
Scott County, Missouri, 1942.

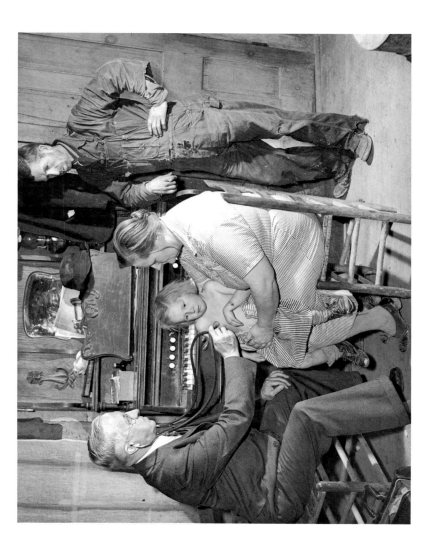

47. Russell Lee. FSA clients at home,
Hidalgo County, Texas, 1939.

48. John Vachon. Boys in front of a drugstore,
Dover, Delaware, 1938.

49. Dorothea Lange. Street Meeting,
San Francisco, California, 1936.

ORGANIZATIONS
FIGHT
Against
IMPERIALIST
DEMAND
AMERICAN
PRESS
SLANDER
Hitler's Nazis
Agents of the German Bosses

50. Ben Shahn. Citizens of Columbus, Ohio, 1938.

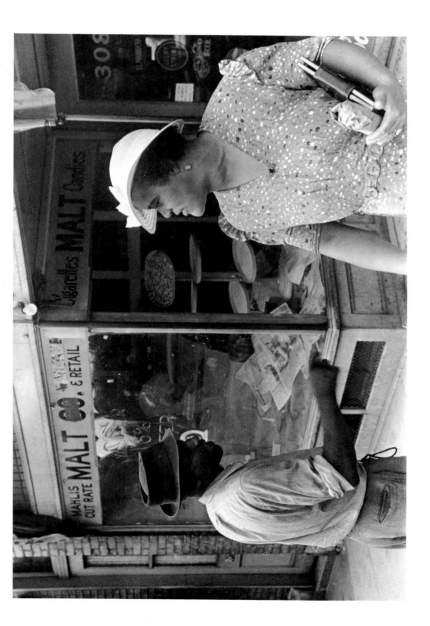

51. Russell Lee. Two negro men playing a game of "Coon-Can" in a store, Reserve, Louisiana, 1938.

52. Walker Evans. Billboard, Birmingham, Alabama, 1936.

53. Jack Delano. In the convict camp in Greene County, Georgia, 1941.

54. Russell Lee. Office of the train dispatcher and Western Union, San Augustine, Texas, 1939.

55. Russell Lee. In front of the movie theater,
Chicago, Illinois, 1941.

56. Walker Evans. Filling station and company houses
for miners, vicinity Morgantown, West Virginia, 1935.

57. Walker Evans. Billboards and frame houses,
Atlanta, Georgia, 1936.

58. John Vachon. Traveling salesman in hotel lobby,
Elkins, West Virginia, 1939.

59. Ben Shahn. Street scene, Lancaster, Ohio, 1938.

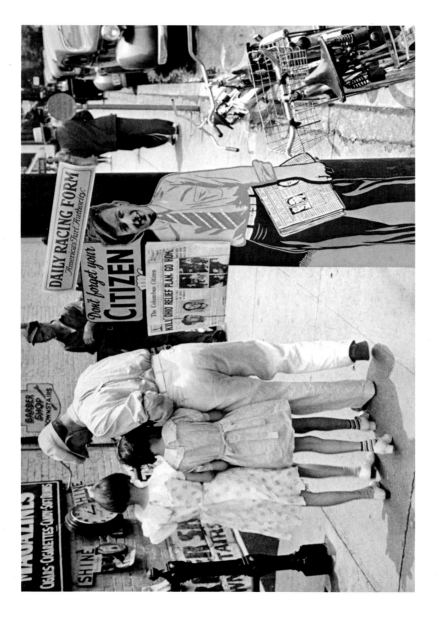

60. Jack Delano. A woman sitting in an automobile,
Franklin, Georgia, 1941.

61. Walker Evans. Graveyard, houses and steel mill,
Bethlehem, Pennsylvania, 1935.

BIOGRAPHY

John Collier, 1913.

Attended California School of Fine Arts intending to become a painter. Through his childhood friend Dorothea Lange he became interested in photography.

He worked on a personal project documenting a typical Mexican-American sheep camp in the Southwest and showed the photos to Lange. Upon her suggestion he sent them to Stryker in Washington. He then went to work for a commercial photographer in San Franciso until Stryker sent word that he would like him to join the FSA. He was the last photographer hired for this section. Collier traveled throughout New England and the South. When the FSA was absorbed by the office of War Information, Collier stayed on until he joined the Merchant Marine for the duration of the war. Later he rejoined Stryker at Standard Oil and then went on to do commercial photography for various magazines. Since 1955 he has become involved with the use of photography as a means of better understanding human behavior and produced his book *Visual Anthropology.*

He is presently associated with San Francisco State University School of Anthropology and teaches creative photography at San Francisco Art Institute.

Bibliography

Collier, John Jr. *Visual Anthropology: Photography as a Research Method.* New York, Holt Rinehart & Winston, Inc. 1967.

Jack Delano, 1914.

Born in Russia, his family emigrated to the U.S. and settled in Pennsylvania. After graduating from high school he attended Pennsylvania Academy of Fine Arts and was awarded a Cresson Traveling Fellowship in 1936. With this

he left for Europe, purchased a small camera and began photographing. In 1939, he became a full-time photographer and photographed coal mining conditions in Schuylkill County, Pennsylvania, for Federal Arts Project. He moved to New York City and became a staff photographer for the United Fund. In spring 1940 he joined the FSA and eventually traveled up and down the Atlantic Coast. He was requested to go on a trip to Puerto Rico in fall 1941 as a favor for a political appointee.

Due to the outbreak of the war in December he was unable to get back to the United States. He stayed on and photographed the island which later became his home. Besides continuing in photography (including assignments for Stryker when he was at Standard Oil) he composes music, designs books (with his wife until her death in 1982) and was at one time general manager of the government's TV and Radio Services.

Walker Evans, 1903-1975.

Born in Saint Louis, Missouri. He moved with his family to Chicago. After his parents divorced, he moved with his mother to New York. He continued his education at Phillips Academy, Andover, and from 1922-23 attended Williams University. Evans returned to New York City and found a job in the public library but in 1926 moved to Paris to audit classes at the Sorbonne. In 1927 he returned to the United States. In 1928, possibly as a rebellion against a commercially-oriented society, he began photo-graphy with a vest-pocket camera. Living in Greenwich Village, Evans met and was influenced by such intellectuals, writers and painters as Lincoln Kirsten, Hart Crane, Ben Shahn and James Agee. During that period he illustrated Hart Crane's book of poems, *The Bridge* (1930), Carleton Beal's book *The Crime of Cuba* (1933) and documented the Museum of

Modern Art's exhibit "African Negro Art" (1935). In October 1935 he joined the photographic unit of the Resettlement Administration. He traveled to Pennsylvania, West Virginia, Alabama, Mississippi, Louisiana and Georgia, making his extremely direct, seemingly straightforward photos which were yet a detailed description of the subject he portrayed. On a leave of absence from the FSA in 1936, Evans worked on a project for *Fortune* with his friend James Agee. The assignment was to do an article on the daily life of a white tenant family in the Deep South. They settled in Hale County, Alabama, during July and August 1936 and worked with three families. The resulting work, though refused by *Fortune,* resulted in the classical work *Let Us Now Praise Famous Men.* Evans stayed with the FSA until 1937 when Stryker fired him. This was his most sustained creative period and he made among the finest group of photos in the file. He was awarded a Guggenheim fellowship in 1941. Evans joined the staff of *Time* magazine in 1943, transferred to *Fortune* in 1945 as a writer/photographer, and stayed until 1965. In that same year he joined the faculty of Yale University as a professor of graphic design. He retired in 1971.

Bibliography

Agee, James & Walker Evans. *Let Us Now Praise Famous Men: Three Tenant Families.* Boston, Houghton Mifflin, reprinted 1960.
Louons maintenant les grands hommes. Paris, Plon, 1972.

Evans, Walker. *Many Are Called.* Essay by James Agee. Boston, Houghton Mifflin, 1960.

Evans, Walker. *American Photographs.* Essay by Lincoln Kirstein. New York, The Museum of Modern Art, reprinted 1962.

Walker Evans. Introduction by John Szarkowski. New York, The Museum of Modern Art, 1971.

Walker Evans: Photographs for the Farm Security Administration 1935-1938. Introduction by

Jerald C. Maddox. New York, Da Capo Press, 1974.

Walker Evans: First and Last. New York, Harper & Row, 1977.

Walker Evans. Introduction by Robert Coles. Aperture History of Photography, Series, vol. 12. Millerton, New York, Aperture, 1980.

Walker Evans At Work. Introduction by Jerry L. Thompson. New York, Harper & Row, 1982.

Theo Jung, 1906.

Born in Vienna, his family emigrated to Chicago in 1912. In 1916 he obtained his first camera. Jung was influenced by the photos of Eugène Atget, August Sander and André Kertész. In February 1934 he took a job with the Federal Relief Administration in Washington, D.C., preparing charts with pictorial statistics on unemployment. He continued taking photos and submitted his portfolio to Stryker. He was hired in September 1935 to work for the FSA and remained there until May 1936 when there was a budget cut. He had worked in Maryland, Indiana and Ohio. In 1937 he joined the Consumers Council as an art director and photographer for the Consumers Guide. He entered into private business as art director/photographer for several publications and avertising agencies. Interested in book design and calligraphy, he won many awards for book and publication design. His interest in photography still continues. He is currently retired and living in Palo Alto, California.

Dorothea Lange, 1895-1965.

Born in Hoboken, New Jersey, and educated in the New York City public schools.
From 1914-17 she attended the New York Training School for Teachers. In 1915 she decided to become a photographer and visited Arnold Genthe who presented her with her first camera. She studied photography

with Clarence White at Columbia University from 1917-18. She decided to leave New York to travel and work her way around the world but her trip ended abruptly in San Francisco. There she found work in a camera store and in 1919 opened her own portrait studio. The following year she married painter Maynard Dixon and throughout the Twenties raised a family, accompanied her husband on his painting trips and continued taking portrait photos. Observing conditions caused by the Depression in the early 1930 she took her camera to the streets to photograph people, hoping to make the public aware of what was happening.

These new photos exhibited by Willard Van Dyke struck Paul S. Taylor, economics professor at California University as important social documents.

He convinced Lange to work with him, using her photos in a report on the plight of migrant workers. In 1935 she and Taylor were married. Because of this work she was asked to join the FSA in 1935 where she worked steadily until 1937. After that she worked on and off for the FSA until 1942. During this time she traveled in the South, Southwest and the Pacific Northwest taking pictures that allowed the human condition to speak for itself. In 1941 she received a Guggenheim fellowship. During World War II, she worked with the Office of War Information and the War Relocation Authority photographing the Japanese-Americans being evacuated from the Pacific Coast.

Lange fell ill in 1945 and did not begin to photograph again before 1951. Then she did such photographic essays as "Mormon Village" (with Ansel Adams), "The Irish Country-woman" and "The Public Defender" for *Life* magazine in 1954 and 1955. In 1958 she traveled with her husband to Asia and in 1963 to Egypt. Lange died in 1965 while working on a retrospective exhibition for the Museum of Modern Art in NYC.

Bibliography

Dorothea Lange. Introduction by George P. Elliot. New York, the Museum of Modern Art, 1966.

Lange, Dorothea. *Dorothea Lange Looks at the American Country Woman.* Introduction by Beaumont Newhall. Forth Worth, Amon Carter Museum, 1967.

Lange, Dorothea and Paul S. Taylor. *An American Exodus: A Record of Human Erosion.* Reprinted from 1939 edition. New York, Arno Press, 1975.

Meltzer, Milton. *Dorothea Lange. A Photographer's Life.* New York, Farrar, Strauss & Giroux, 1978.

Dorothea Lange: Farm Security Administration Photographs, 1935-1939. 2 vols. Glencoe, Illinois, the Text-Fiche Press, 1980.

Ohrn, Karin B. *Dorothea Lange and the Documentary Tradition* Baton Rouge, Louisiana State University Press, 1980.

Photos by Dorothea Lange. Aperture History of Photography Series. Vol. 17. Millerton, New York, Aperture, 1981.

Coles, Robert. *Dorothea Lange: Photographs of a Lifetime.* Millerton, New York, Aperture, 1982.

Russell Lee, 1903.

Born and raised in Illinois. After the divorce of his parents and then the death of his mother, Lee was raised by his grandparents and later on by a series of legal guardians. He graduated from Lehigh University in 1925 with a degree in chemical engineering and began work in Illinois making composition roofing. In 1928, he was promoted to plant manager and he moved with his painter wife to Kansas City.

He found the job boring and as he had independent means, decided to leave and become a painter. The Lees moved to San Francisco and in 1931, upon a suggestion from a friend, moved to an artists colony in Woodstock, New York. They stayed on until 1935, spending winters in NYC where Lee studied at the Art Students' League. Hoping to help improve his drawing, Lee bought a little 35 mm Contax in 1935 and soon his interest in photography surpassed that of art. He heard about the photography being done by the Resettlement Administration and he had his agent submit his portfolio to Stryker. Shortly thereafter Mydans left the FSA and Lee was offered his place. In September 1936 he became part of the section. Traveling with his second wife he extensively covered the Midwest and the West making his well-known "Pie Town" New Mexico and "San Augustine" series.

He continued with the Historical Section until 1942 when he joined the Office of War Information. In 1943 he was commissioned Captain in the Air Transport Command. After the war he was photographer for a medical survey conducted in 1946-47 by the Coal Mines Administration. The result was an illustrated report, *A Medical Survey of the Bituminous Coal Industry,* published by the Department of the Interior in 1947. A smaller heavily illustrated supplement, *The Coal Miner and His Family,* was distributed among miners and mine owners. In 1947 the Lees settled in Austin, Texas. He did some industrial assignments, some of them for Stryker who was then at Standard Oil of New Jersey. In 1948-62 Lee was associated with the University of Missouri Photo Workshop. In 1965 he joined the faculty of the University of Texas and retired in 1973.

Bibliography

Hurley, F. Jack. *Russell Lee Photographer.* Dobbs Ferry, New York, Morgan and Morgan, 1978.

Russell Lee: Farm Security Administration Photographs, 1936-1942. 2 vol. Glencoe, Illinois, the Text-Fiche Press, 1983.

Carl Mydans, 1907.

Graduated from the School of Journalism at Boston University in 1930. During his studies he worked part-time as a writer for the *Boston Globe* and the *Boston Herald.* Though he used a camera he did not consider himself a photographer.

In 1931, joined staff of the *American Banker,* a small New York City daily.

He bought his first 35 mm camera, a Contax, and began doing free-lance photography selling his prints primarily to *Time* magazine. He was hired by the Resettlement Administration to produce a book about suburban resettlement but the project was never completed. At the end of 1935 Mydans was reassigned to Stryker's Historical Section and he traveled to the South and New England. He left in October 1936 to join the staff of the newly created *Life* magazine becoming an outstanding photojournalist. He headed the *Time-Life* Bureau in Tokyo after the war. For his coverage of the Korean War in 1950 he received the U.S. Camera Gold Achievement Award. Continues to be a part of *Time-Life* to this day.

Bibliography

Mydans, Carl. *More than Meets the Eye.* Reprinted from the 1959 edition. Westport, Connecticut, Greenwood Press, 1974.

Marion Post Wolcott, 1910.

Post Wolcott became interested in photography while studying at University of Vienna.

She returned to U.S. and began teaching at Hessian Hills School in Croton-on-the-Hudson and while there began first commercial work taking portraits of school children. She left teaching to concentrate on photography, selling her photos to *Vogue, Life* and *Fortune.* In 1937 she became staff photographer for the Philadelphia *Evening Bulletin.* She joined FSA in September 1938 and remained with the program until the end doing the bulk of her work in the South. Mrs. Wolcott resigned in 1942 to raise a family but began to photograph again in 1976.

Arthur Rothstein, 1915.

Born and raised in New York, he attended Columbia University where one of his professors was Stryker. He did copy and print work for one of Stryker's projects. Upon graduation, though intent upon pursuing further studies in chemistry or medicine, he accepted instead an offer by Stryker to join the Resettlement Administration. He was the first person hired and worked with the section from 1935-40. He initially set up the darkroom and began to photograph. He was impressed by the photos of Evans, Lange and Shahn. Rothstein traveled more than the others all over the United States (Oklahoma, South Dakota, Washington, Montana, the Midwest, New England and the South). In 1940 he joined *Look* magazine but left to join the Office of War Information and then the army. He served as chief photographer for the United Nations Relief and Rehabilitation Administration in China. He rejoined *Look* in 1946 as technical director of photography and was appointed director of photography in 1969. He became editor of *Infinity* magazine in 1971. He was visual aids consultant to the U.S. Environmental Protection Agency and the American Iron and Steel Institute. Presently Rothstein is an associate editor of *Parade,* a Sunday newspaper magazine. He is also a member of the Graduate School of Columbia University and a founder and former officer of the American Society of Magazine Photographers.

Bibliography

Rothstein, Arthur. *Creative Color in Photography.* Philadelphia, Chilton, 1963.

Rothstein, Arthur. *Color Photography Now.* New York, American Photographic Book Publishing Co., 1970.

Rothstein, Arthur. *The Depression Years: As Photographed by Arthur Rothstein.* New York, Dover, 1978.

Rothstein, Arthur. *Photojournalism: Pictures for Magazines and Newspapers.* New York, American Photograhic Book Publishing Co., 4th edition, 1979.

Rothstein, Arthur. *Arthur Rothstein: His Words and Pictures.* New York,

American Photographic Book Publishing Co., 1979.

Rothstein, Arthur. *The American West in the Thirties: One Hundred Twenty-two Photographs.* New York, Dover, 1981.

Ben Shahn, 1898-1969.

Born in Kovno, Lithuania. His family emigrated to America in 1906 and settled in Brooklyn. He apprenticed to a lithographer in 1913 and studied at National Academy of Design in 1922. He traveled in Europe and North Africa (1925; 1927-29). In the 1930's he developed as a painter of social realism. In 1931-32 he exhibited his first social protest canvases on the theme of the Sacco-Vanzetti case followed by a series on Tom Mooney in 1933. In 1935 he enrolled in the government-sponsored PWA (Public Works of Art) project and was brought into the Special Skills Division of the Resettlement Administration as an artist. Probably due to his friendship with Walker Evans, Shahn was asked to join the Historical Section of the RA. It was Evans who had introduced Shahn to photography. Photography for him was a way of notetaking for his future paintings but perhaps because of a special kind of social awareness, he had a way of catching people in their lives. Shahn stayed with the FSA from 1935-38 traveling throughout the South and to Ohio. He returned to painting after leaving the FSA. In 1956 he held the Charles Eliot Norton chair of Poetics at Harvard.

Bibliography

Rodman, Selden. *Portrait of the Artist as an American. Ben Shahn: A Biography with Pictures.* New York, Harper & Bros., 1951.

Ben Shahn, Photographer. An Album from the Thirties. Edited by Margaret R. Weiss. New York, Da Capo Press, 1973.

The Photographic Eye of Ben Shahn. Cambridge, Mass., Harvard University Press, 1975.

John Vachon, 1914-1975.

After doing graduate work in Washington, D.C., he began work as a messenger for the Resettlement Administration in 1936. In April 1937 Ben Shahn gave him some basic instructions on operating a camera and he began to photograph street scenes in Washington, D.C. Walker Evans taught him how to operate an 8"x10" view camera.
He received his first real FSA assignment in October 1938 and in 1940 officially became an FSA photographer and traveled through the Great Plains, the Midwest, Maryland, West Virginia and Kentucky. He continued to work for the FSA until 1942 when he went to work for the OWI which absorbed the Historical Section. After military service, he worked primarily for *Look* magazine and taught photography. He received a Guggenheim Fellowship in 1973-74 to do a study of North Dakota in winter.

Bibliography

John Vachon: Farm Security Administration Photographs, 1938-1942. Glencoe, Illinois, the Text-Fiche Press, 1982.

GENERAL BIBLIOGRAPHY

The Bitter Years 1934-41: Rural America as Seen by the Photographers of the Farm Security Administration. Edited by Edward Steichen with an introduction by Grace M. Meyer. New York, The Museum of Modern Art, 1962.

Just Before the War. Edited by Thomas H. Garver. Balboa, California, Newport Harbor Art Museum, 1968.

Hurley, F. Jack. *Portrait of a Decade: Roy Stryker and the Development of Documentary Photography in the Thirties.* Baton Rouge, Louisiana State University Press, 1972.

Stryker, Roy Emerson and Nancy Wood, *In This Proud Land. America 1935-1943, as Seen in the F.S.A. Photographs.* Greenwich, Connecticut, New York Graphic Society, Ltd., 1973.

The Years of Bitterness and Pride. F.S.A. Photographs 1935-1943. New York, McGraw-Hill Book Company, 1975.

O'Neal, Hank. *A Vision Shared, A Classic Portrait of America and It's People, 1935-1943.* New York, St Martin's Press, 1976.

PHOTOFILE

The Photofile series is conceived and produced
by the Centre National de la Photographie, Paris,
under the direction of Robert Delpire.